W9-DHI-108

Native American Biographies

CHIEF TECUMSEH

Anne M. Todd

Heinemann Library
Chicago, Illinois

Customer Service   888–454–2279

Visit our website at www.heinemannlibrary.com

Designed by Kim Saar/Heinemann Library
Maps by John Fleck
Photo research by Alan Gottlieb
Printed in China by WKT Company Limited

08 07 06 05 04
10 9 8 7 6 5 4 3 2 1

Library of Congress Cataloging-in-Publication Data
Todd, Anne M.
  Chief Tecumseh / Anne M. Todd.
    p. cm. -- (Native American biographies)
  Summary: A biography of Tecumseh, chief of the Shawnee people during the late 1700s, describing the battles the Shawnee fought against the white people, as well as the Battle of Tippecanoe, where Tecumseh fought for the British during the War of 1812.
  Includes bibliographical references and index.
  ISBN 1-4034-5002-1 (lib. bdg.) -- ISBN 1-4034-5009-9 (pbk.)
  1. Tecumseh, Shawnee Chief, 1768-1813--Juvenile literature. 2. Shawnee Indians--Kings and rulers--Biography--Juvenile literature. 3. Shawnee Indians--Wars--Juvenile literature. 4. United States--History--War of 1812--Juvenile literature. [1. Tecumseh, Shawnee Chief, 1768-1813. 2. Shawnee Indians--Biography. 3. Indians of North America--East (U.S.)--Biography. 4. Kings, queens, rulers, etc.] I. Title. II. Series: Native American biographies (Heinemann Library (Firm))
  E99.S35T467 2004
  977.004'973'0092--dc22
                                    2003020489

Acknowledgments
The author and publisher are grateful to the following for permission to reproduce copyright material:
p. 5 Library of Congress/Neg. #LC-USZC4-3616; p. 7 Clark County Historical Society; pp. 8, 11, 18, 19 Ohio Historical Society; p. 9 Southeastern Architectural Archive/Tulane University Library; p. 10 Ben Klaffke; p. 13 Library of Congress/Neg. # LC-USZC4-4913; p. 14 Stapleton Collection/Corbis; p. 17 David Wright/Greystone Press; p. 20 Cincinnati Historical Society and Museum Center; p. 21 Chicago Historical Society; p. 23 Hulton Archive/Getty Images; p. 24 National Portrait Gallery, Smithsonian Institution/Art Resource, NY; pp. 25, 26 Bettmann/Corbis; p. 27 Kevin Cullen/Lafayette Journal and Courier; p. 28 Smithsonian American Art Museum/Art Resource, NY; p. 29 Courtesy National Congress of American Indians

Cover photographs by (foreground) Hulton Archive/Getty Images (background) Robert Lifson/Heinemann Library

Special thanks to Chief Charles D. Enyart of the Eastern Shawnee Tribe and to the Shawnee Tribe for their help in the preparation of this book.

The image of Chief Tecumseh on the cover of this book was painted around 1790 by Mathais Noheimer. The background shows a river in eastern Ohio.

Contents

▶ Some words are shown in bold, **like this.** You can
▶ find out what they mean by looking in the glossary.

One Man's Dream

Tecumseh was a Shawnee Indian leader who wanted peace. He wanted to stop the fighting between the American Indians and the United States government. He wanted his people to have a safe home where they could hunt and live peacefully.

Tecumseh felt that all Indians should work together to protect their lands.

Tecumseh traveled to talk to Indians of all **tribes.**
When he spoke, people listened. Tecumseh was tall,
handsome, and spoke with energy. He believed that
if Indians worked together, they could stop white
people from taking away their land.

In Their Own Words

"Brothers, we all belong to one family. We are all children of the Great **Spirit.** We walk the same path. . . We must fight each other's battles."

—Tecumseh

Growing Up Shawnee

Tecumseh was probably born in 1768 near the Shawnee town of Old Piqua in present-day Ohio. In the late 1700s, most Shawnees lived in parts of present-day Indiana, Michigan, Ohio, and Canada. Most Shawnee villages, like Old Piqua, were located near rivers.

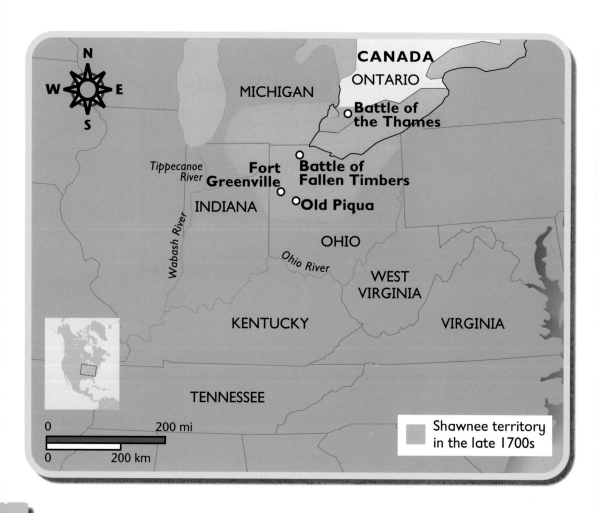

Tecumseh's father, Pukeshinwau, and his mother, Methoataaskee, were Shawnee Indians. Tecumseh had many brothers and sisters. His oldest brother's name was Cheeseekau. His youngest brother was later known as Tenskwatawah.

Tecumseh's Name

When he was about six months old, Tecumseh's name was chosen at a **ceremony.** An **elder** chose his name.

The town where Tecumseh grew up was located near the Mad River in present-day Ohio. This modern photograph shows the area near the Mad River.

While Tecumseh was growing up, there was much fighting between the Shawnees and the white **settlers** and military. The settlers wanted to live on Shawnee land. The Shawnees fought to keep this land.

This painting shows Cornstalk, a Shawnee leader. Cornstalk fought against the settlers while Tecumseh was growing up.

When Tecumseh was six years old, his father and his oldest brother, Cheeseekau, left with a group of Shawnees to fight for their land. During the battle, Tecumseh's father died. Tecumseh's oldest sister, Tecumapease, and Cheeseekau took care of Tecumseh.

Tecumapease

Tecumapease was like a second mother to Tecumseh. She taught Tecumseh to be truthful and honest. She gave him love and support as he became a teenager.

In Tecumseh's time, Shawnee hunting camps looked like this one. The painting was made in 1820.

Cheeseekau taught Tecumseh how to hunt and fight. Tecumseh learned to recognize different animal sounds. He and the other Shawnee boys played games that would help them become **warriors.**

Today most Shawnee children live in Oklahoma.

Tecumseh liked to be a leader. He would split the boys into two teams. Then they would pretend to fight. Tecumseh's team usually came away with a victory.

Timeline

Tecumseh was born	Pukeshinwau died in battle
1768	1774

This is a **ceremonial** pipe. Tecumseh gave it to a member of the Ohio state congress in 1807.

Becoming a Warrior

As Tecumseh grew older, he began to go into battle with Cheeseekau. Sometimes Shawnees **tortured** prisoners from the battles. Tecumseh did not like this. He spoke against it when he was older.

Joseph Brant lived from 1742 to 1807.

During this time, Tecumseh heard about a Mohawk Iroquois leader, Joseph Brant. Like other American Indians had done before him, Brant was working to form a **confederacy.** He wanted Indian people of all **tribes** to get together to fight off the **settlers.** Tecumseh would remember this idea later in his life.

Treaty of Fort Harmar

In 1789 the Shawnee lost nearly all of the land in present-day Ohio to the United States. This was called the **Treaty** of Fort Harmar. Tecumseh worked hard the rest of his life trying to regain this land. He wanted the Ohio River to form a boundary between settlers and Indians.

Tecumseh quickly became a skilled **warrior.** He had great courage. He traveled to places where Indians were fighting the white **settlers** and military. Over the next several years, Tecumseh became a leader of Shawnee warriors.

Fighting for Their Land

In 1791 a group of Shawnees attacked United States soldiers. The soldiers, led by Arthur St. Clair, were trying to push the Indians out of present-day Ohio. The Indians won the battle. This victory encouraged Tecumseh and other warriors. They hoped that they could stay in Ohio.

Tecumseh was also successful off the battlefield. He was known as a kind and generous person. Returning from a hunt, he gave most of the meat to people in need. This was a **tradition** among Shawnee hunters. Tecumseh got along well with people. He laughed easily and liked to make jokes.

Arthur St. Clair left the army a year after he was defeated by the Shawnees.

In 1792 Tecumseh and his brother Cheeseekau traveled to Tennessee with about forty other Shawnee **warriors.** The Shawnees fought alongside Creek and Cherokee Indians to stop more **settlers** from entering Tennessee. Together, there were about 400 Indians.

In Their Own Words

"Tecumseh [was] proud, courageous, and high-spirited. . . [He] would never yield. . . [He] would any time fight double his number."

—Anthony Shane,
who grew up among the Shawnees

Shawnees hunted with guns after the arrival of European settlers in the 1700s.

During the battle, a soldier shot and killed Cheeseekau. Tecumseh was greatly saddened by his brother's death. Cheeseekau had been like a father to Tecumseh. He had taught Tecumseh how to be a brave warrior. He was also Tecumseh's good friend.

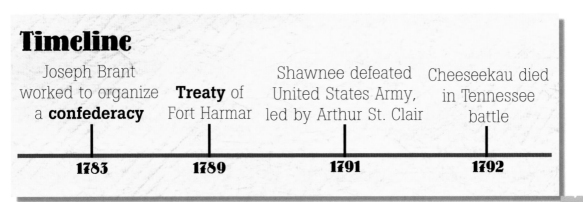

Timeline

Joseph Brant worked to organize a **confederacy**	**Treaty** of Fort Harmar	Shawnee defeated United States Army, led by Arthur St. Clair	Cheeseekau died in Tennessee battle
1783	1789	1791	1792

Standing Alone

The United States President, George Washington, decided the **settlers** in Ohio needed protection from Indians. He ordered an army to make the Ohio Indians leave the state. This army was led by Major-General Anthony Wayne.

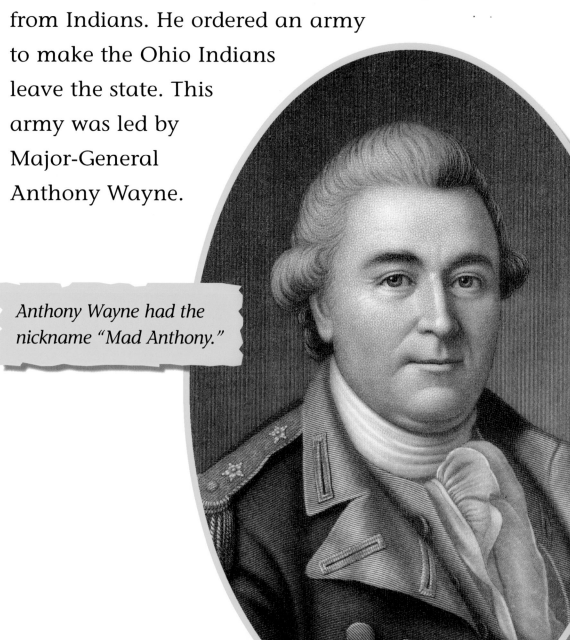

Anthony Wayne had the nickname "Mad Anthony."

At the Battle of Fallen Timbers, Tecumseh led his people against Wayne's soldiers. Tecumseh fought with great courage. But there were more United States soldiers than Indian **warriors.** Tecumseh and his people had to **retreat.**

Dressing for Battle

When preparing for battle, Tecumseh did not decorate his body much. Usually, he painted a single red line around his hair. For important battles, he wore more paint. He painted his whole face red.

The Battle of Fallen Timbers happened in 1794 near present-day Toledo, Ohio.

In 1795 an important meeting took place at Fort Greenville in present-day Ohio. Many Indian leaders were there. Tecumseh was not. He was hunting and did not want to sign the **Treaty** of Greenville. The treaty stated that the United States government would pay Indians for the land in Ohio. It also promised yearly payments of money.

Ninety-one American Indians signed the Treaty of Greenville.

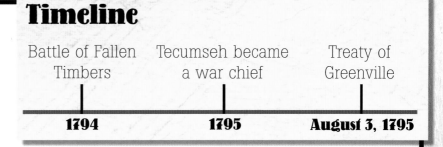

Timeline

Battle of Fallen Timbers	Tecumseh became a war chief	Treaty of Greenville
1794	1795	August 3, 1795

By this time Tecumseh had become a war chief by showing his leadership and courage in battle. Around 1797 Tecumseh and a group of about 250 of his followers moved to Indiana.

Many Shawnees respected Tecumseh for not signing the Treaty of Greenville.

Strength Together

People today are only certain of Tecumseh having one son. This son moved west in the 1800s. Later, Tecumseh's grandson became the leader of the Absentee Shawnee **Tribe** in present-day Oklahoma.

In Their Own Words

"No tribe has the right to sell, even to each other, much less to strangers. . . Sell a country! Why not sell the air, the great sea, as well as the earth? Didn't the Great **Spirit** make them all for the use of his children?"

—Tecumseh

Many people believed that the Prophet could perform miracles.

But in the early 1800s Tecumseh's youngest brother, Tenskwatawah, believed that Indians had to return to their **traditions.** He thought Indians should have nothing to do with **settlers.** People came from all tribes to listen to him. Some of them called Tenskwatawah the **Prophet.** Tecumseh had always believed in **uniting** all Indians against the settlers. When people came to listen to the Prophet, Tecumseh took the chance to talk about these beliefs. People listened. Tecumseh and the Prophet worked to bring all Indians together.

Tecumseh and the **Prophet** built a village called Prophetstown where the Wabash and Tippecanoe rivers meet in present-day Indiana. Shawnees and people from other **tribes** gathered at the village. Tecumseh traveled to other states. He told other Indian tribes about their village and their beliefs.

While Tecumseh was away, the United States Army camped near the village. William Henry Harrison had plans to attack. The Prophet was not a **warrior**, but he decided to make a surprise attack on the army. But Harrison's army had twice as many men as the Prophet. The soldiers easily won the battle. This was called the Battle of Tippecanoe.

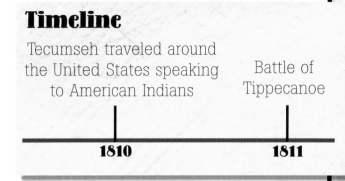

Timeline

Tecumseh traveled around the United States speaking to American Indians

Battle of Tippecanoe

1810

1811

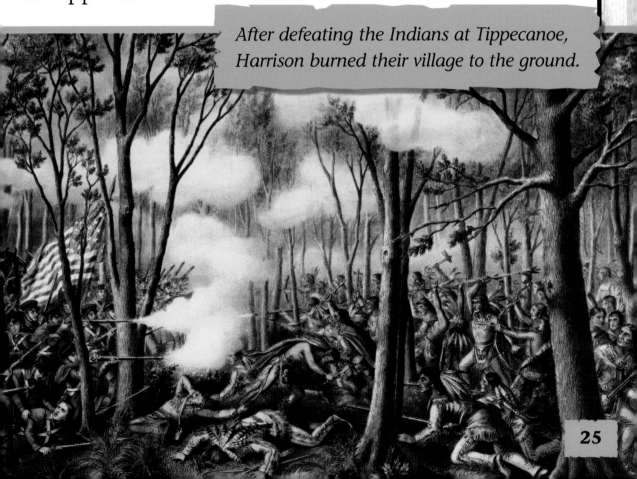

After defeating the Indians at Tippecanoe, Harrison burned their village to the ground.

The End of the Battle

Tecumseh's people moved to the villages of other Shawnees. Then the United States declared war on Great Britain. This was called the War of 1812. Tecumseh hoped that Great Britain would win the war and return land to the Indians. Tecumseh became a general for the British army.

The Battle of Thames was fought in Canada on October 5, 1813.

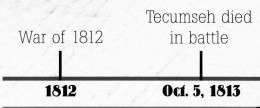
War of 1812

Tecumseh died in battle

1812

Oct. 5, 1813

Tecumseh and his army led many successful attacks against the United States. Then he faced the man who had destroyed his village, William Henry Harrison. Harrison's army fought Tecumseh's army at the Battle of the Thames. Tecumseh was shot and killed during the battle.

This memorial marks the place where the Battle of Tippecanoe was fought. It was built in 1908.

In Their Own Words

"Our lives are in the hands of the Great **Spirit.**
We are determined to defend our lands, and if it
is his will, we wish to leave our bones upon them."
— Tecumseh

A Life Remembered

The United States won the War of 1812. The war put an end to Tecumseh's **confederacy.** He had tried to bring peace and **unity** for all Indians. He spoke about living in peace alongside whites. He wanted his people to be free. He wanted them to live as they wanted—not how the United States government wanted them to live.

This statue of Tecumseh can be seen at the National Museum of American Art in Washington, D.C.

The NCAI brings people's attention to issues that are important to all American Indians.

Today many Indian **organizations** support American Indian unity. One example is the National Congress of American Indians (NCAI). The NCAI gives **tribal** leaders from all Indian groups a chance to voice their concerns. Through organizations like this one, Tecumseh's idea of Indian unity continues today.

Glossary

ceremony   event that celebrates a special occasion

confederacy   different groups of people coming
together for a common purpose

elder   older person, such as grandparent, who is
treated with respect

miracle   something very rare, unusual,
or wonderful

organization   group of people who work together
for a common purpose

prophet   spiritual leader who can predict events
in the future

retreat   run away from a battle

settler   person who makes a home in a new place

spirit   invisible force or being with special power

torture   cause great pain to a prisoner

tradition   custom or story that has been passed
from older people to younger people for a
long time

treaty   agreement between governments or groups of people

tribe   group of people who share language, customs, beliefs, and often government

unite   come together to do something

warrior   person who fights in battles

More Books to Read

Fitterer, C. Ann. *Tecumseh: Chief of the Shawnee*. Eden Prairie, Minn.: The Child's World, 2002.

Koestler-Grack, Rachel A. *Tecumseh: 1768–1813*. Minnetonka, Minn.: Capstone Press, 2002.

Yacowitz, Caryn. *Shawnee Indians*. Chicago: Heinemann Library, 2003.

Index